SALLY FOLEY-LEWIS

SUCCESSFUL FEEDBACK

HOW LEADERS CAN INCREASE PERFORMANCE, MOTIVATE AND ENGAGE THEIR TEAM

"Prior to having EECC in my toolkit, I found it difficult to know where to begin when having challenging conversations with colleagues. More often than not, these conversations were not effective because I would discuss things that weren't relevant or useful in working towards a solution. The EECC formula was effective for me as it provided me with a simple, repeatable and realistic framework that I have found easy to apply in my work setting."
– Carly Hislop, Team Leader, Townsville Hospital & Health Service

"I loved reading Sally's book, *Successful Feedback*, as it was short, informative and straight to the point. Sally's EECC feedback formula is an amazing guideline on how you can give positive and corrective feedback while also encouraging the person on the other end to contribute to the discussion on how they can perform better. After reading the book, I tried using EECC when I had to address my colleague about a problem that started reoccurring often. My colleague took the whole thing well and even commented on how he will take more care when doing that certain task. I found it so effective that I still use it today whenever I can."
– TraMi Huvnh, Scientific Officer, Austech Medical Laboratories

"I have found using the feedback formula makes difficult conversations much easier. When people are aware of the effect of their actions, it is easier for them to change and commit to the change. I have used the feedback formula both in positive and negative situations with very good results."
– G. White, Manager

"I have started reading your book and it has already given me cause to stop and think about how I give feedback. So far, the bit that hit me was the planning bit. Sometimes I give feedback on the run – now, I feel that comes across as telling, not being interested in what the other person might have to say."
– B. Kelly, business owner

"Buy this for your boss! Sally Foley-Lewis is an expert in the field of management – high-performance management. She has delivered a simple and powerful approach to giving feedback that empowers both the giver and the receiver. It's simple and easy to implement – and it works. Just check out her LinkedIn recommendations from delighted clients for proof. Buy *Successful Feedback* for your team's sake. They will love you for it."
– Robin Dickinson, Consultant

Have you ever been on the rough end of feedback?
Have you ever avoided *that* awkward conversation?
Have you started a feedback conversation on a positive note,
then suddenly, from what seems out of nowhere, there are tears,
blame, anger and frustration?

You are not alone!

Feedback needs structure.

Feedback conversations can be easy.

Feedback is a human process not a paperwork task.

Let this book be your guide!

For you …

ABOUT SALLY FOLEY-LEWIS

Sally Foley-Lewis has spent the past 20 years coaching and mentoring people to become more productive. She develops leaders' efficiency by building their people and team skills, improving their task management and nurturing their self-leadership. She works with middle managers and team leaders in large corporates and associations in Australia and overseas, as well as employers in small to medium-sized businesses.

Essentially, she is a productivity and leadership expert.

Obsessed with execution, Sally enables people to not only get on with their work but with their peers, senior leaders and teams. The flow-on effect of this is profound: leaders witness an even greater level of engagement and productivity from their team members.

What makes Sally different to other coaches is that she, too, has been a manager and CEO. She knows first-hand the pressure of balancing your own workload, leading a team and delivering the required outcomes. Sally has experienced the struggle of life in the trenches, so she truly gets it!

Sally has also trained and developed managers and leaders across a diverse range of industries in Australia and overseas. Her unique skillset and depth of experience mean she knows how to make real, lasting improvements to productivity, leadership and performance. It's a journey.

As a leader, working with different people means managing, influencing and manoeuvering different personalities. You may be avoiding certain conversations that deep down you know you should have, but you're unsure how to start or you're afraid of the ramifications. If you look at your team members' performance and you feel overwhelmed and stuck with how to handle performance conversations, let alone get through the annual review paperwork, it can impact the way you lead your team. It can even be a challenge to work out how to praise team members in a way that feels authentic, genuine and not tokenistic. Being in this situation can impact your ability to achieve what's required.

Sally understands this. She can help you begin the conversations you need to have so you can move forward. She can help you work through your fears, take control of your leadership and be excited about your work.

Sally speaks, mentors, trains and coaches in the areas of feedback, productivity and leadership. She does this through workshops, presentations and mentoring for leaders who want to build their skills and confidence so they can lead their teams more effectively – by delegating appropriately, leading difficult conversations with confidence, and giving feedback in ways that effect positive change.

Sally can help you understand the different team roles and behaviours at play and why conflicts arise. More importantly, she teaches you how to resolve them quickly.

To find out more about Sally and her programs, go to www.sallyfoleylewis.com

SALLY FOLEY-LEWIS

An inability to tolerate feedback is an inability to allow yourself personal growth.
– Unknown

I think it's very important to have a feedback loop, where you're constantly thinking about what you've done and how you could be doing it better.
– Elon Musk

SALLY FOLEY-LEWIS

CONTENTS

CONTENTS

It's a big step from criticising what you think is wrong to working out and implementing what you think is right.
– Julia Gillard
Former Australian Prime Minister
Australia's First Female Prime Minister

SALLY FOLEY-LEWIS

INTRODUCTION

Being on the receiving end of no feedback – silence, tumbleweeds – when you're new to an organisation and want to do well is unnerving, to say the least.

Being on the receiving end of vague, flippant praise mixed with backhanded compliments is dirty play and puts you on your guard for what other surprises may be coming your way.

Being on the receiving end of clear, straightforward insights and challenges to assumptions that set clear expectations bolstered by trust and measured support shows you are respected and valued.

These are just three of the many feedback sessions I have experienced as an employee over the years. Some feedback conversations stung and others were challenging, as I felt I needed more support and reassurance. I would leave these conversations wanting more. I also struggled when every effort I employed went unnoticed with zero feedback offered.

When I stepped into my first leadership role and was suddenly on the giving, not just the receiving, end of feedback, these experiences came in handy. Did I instantly become an expert at giving feedback? No! But having experienced the good, the bad and the ugly of feedback ensured that when I stepped in to give feedback, my intentions included helping and focusing on behaviour, rather than getting personal.

Most importantly, I knew my team wanted and needed quality feedback.

Since my first leadership role, I have spent significant time dissecting feedback, exploring what it's truly about and what the real outcomes of feedback should be versus what it tends to be.

Successful Feedback is the how-to guide for ensuring you have the skills, confidence and structure to quickly plan and deliver feedback in an authentic, respectful and open manner. This structure can apply to the informal moments you leverage day-to-day and in the more formal performance-review meetings.

This is not the first *Successful Feedback* book. I wrote an edition in 2012. But this *Successful Feedback* is not a second edition. The topic – the critical skill of feedback – deserved a fresh start. The gems from the quick-read 2012 book are included in this updated version and are accompanied by more insight, support and guidance so you can be an even more confident giver and receiver of feedback.

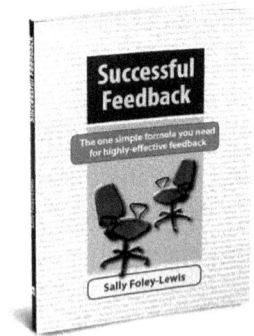

Feedback is an essential skill for any successful leader. When it comes to interpersonal communication skills, so many managers quip, "It's not rocket science!" That's true. Being able to communicate with others in an effective and positive way is not rocket science. However, that doesn't mean it's easy. It's complicated and it can be tricky.

Today, I work with dedicated professionals who know that leadership is a behaviour. And, like all behaviours, they can be learned and improved. The journey of a successful leader includes constantly looking for ways to improve.

I have the great privilege of working with thousands of managers across multiple industries, internationally and in Australia. I'm passionate about helping them to be successful leaders. No matter the geography or culture, common leadership challenges face us all, and feedback is high on that list of challenges.

I'm excited to share this book with you. It matters not what role you're in or what your job title is. *You are a leader.* A leader is not a job title – it's a behaviour. If you have a burning desire to have easier, more effective and influential performance conversations that lead to positive results, this book is for you.

When leaders are prepared to step into conversations that may, at first seem, challenging, and remain calm, focused and results-oriented, they will be better leaders. Your team will thank you for it, even if they never actually say it.

This book is for you if you know you've avoided tough conversations.

This book is for you if you feel giving praise is awkward.

This book is for you if you have given feedback in the past and it's backfired.

This book is for you if you'd like to receive feedback in a more helpful and developmental way.

Enjoy.

Examine what is said and not who speaks.
– African proverb

CHAPTER 1

FEEDBACK - WHAT IS IT REALLY?

1.1 WHAT GOOD FEEDBACK CAN DO FOR YOU, THE TEAM AND THE BOTTOM LINE
1.2 THE 3 AS OF FEEDBACK

> *Is it failure or is it feedback? You choose the view.*
> – Sally Foley-Lewis

Feedback is information for change. Most of the feedback managers give (or are expected to give) is intended to bring about change: improved performance, productivity, amended processes and opportunities to value-add. Giving feedback without a change or action component is simply giving information.

Feedback is a response to performances exhibited and performance expectations.

Corrective feedback – performance that needs improving.
Praise – performance that needs acknowledgement.

According to research by US professional services firm Zenger Folkman in 2014, 57% of respondents preferred feedback that was designed to correct behaviour versus 43% who preferred praise. Additionally, 72% stated they would prefer to receive feedback that provided corrective guidance.

Feedback, be it corrective or praise, needs to build confidence in the individual and the team.

A common employee complaint is that they do not receive any feedback that tells them how well they are doing or where and how they can improve. This lack of feedback quality and quantity results in employee disengagement. And that means employees are not bringing their A-game to work. Their productivity suffers because they have no direction. While you can improve the way you give feedback to your people, consider how you can also improve the way you receive feedback from your employees, peers and senior leaders.

1.1 WHAT GOOD FEEDBACK CAN DO FOR YOU, THE TEAM AND THE BOTTOM LINE

When you give quality feedback, you create a culture of support, respect and clear expectations. This leads to your team understanding:

- Why their role exists.
- What they are meant to achieve.
- What they are doing well and what needs improving.
- What impact their performance has on others in the workplace and on the bottom line.

- What goals are being achieved and which ones are not or need changing.

By having this information, you and your team can co-create a plan of action that is focused, results-driven and engaging.

Poorly delivered feedback has a negative effect on motivation, which impacts focus and goal attainment. Conversely, when time and effort are spent on providing quality feedback – be it corrective or praise – the potential value includes:

- Employees' self-image is enhanced and, therefore, they feel valued and part of something worthwhile.
- As the leader, your role is respected and valued more.
- Productivity increases and improves through clarity of goals and expectations and, as a result, employees use their time more effectively.
- Interpersonal communication improves.
- Trust deepens.
- Resilience as a team improves as individuals can cope with corrective feedback in a more constructive way.

1.2 THE 3 AS OF FEEDBACK

Every quality successful feedback conversation includes the three As:

1. AWARENESS	2. ACTION	3. ACHIEVEMENT
By stating or showing the person what the feedback is (e.g. evidence) and discussing the effect their current performance has on work output, quality, the team, resources, profits, etc., you create insight for the employee. When the employee has a greater awareness of the impact of their performance, it helps them feel a greater responsibility to act. This is not about blame!	Having a greater sense of responsibility to make change – e.g. improvements, amendments, value-adding – means the employee will have an increased willingness to step in and create an action plan. With an action plan, the employee increases their potential for improved focus and increased motivation. Their performance is more likely to change for the better.	As the employee works with their action plan and is supported by you through the process of feedback and accountability, their chances of sustained achievement and success are significantly increased. The organisation, therefore, achieves greater results.

To give some context to the 3 As, consider the opposite effect if feedback didn't aim for awareness, action and achievement:

NEGATIVE EFFECT	POSITIVE EFFECT
Detached	Awareness
Dormant	Action Plan
Defeated	Achievement

No workplace can afford to carry detached, dormant or defeated employees.

SALLY FOLEY-LEWIS

CHAPTER 2

WHY BOTHER ...

Employees who report receiving recognition and praise within the last seven days show increased productivity, get higher scores from customers, and have better safety records.
They're just more engaged at work.
– Tom Rath

... BECAUSE YOUR EMPLOYEES AREN'T ENGAGED WITH THE CURRENT PROCESS

"I say what they want to hear because nothing really happens. I used to get into it and make suggestions, ask for specific training, but nothing ever happened so I don't bother any more."

"Look at this form! It's for an administration worker, I'm a technical specialist. Nothing on this form relates to me. What am I supposed to do with this?"

"We stopped doing annual reviews, which was great because they were awful. The managers were meant to give us feedback regularly but that turned out to be lots of mini awful reviews ... too often. I'd rather

go back to one annual review. The managers here don't really know how to coach and engage me. The managers need training in giving feedback."

"I just want to do my job and be left alone. Why do I have to want to climb the ladder? If I do something wrong, tell me, otherwise leave me be."

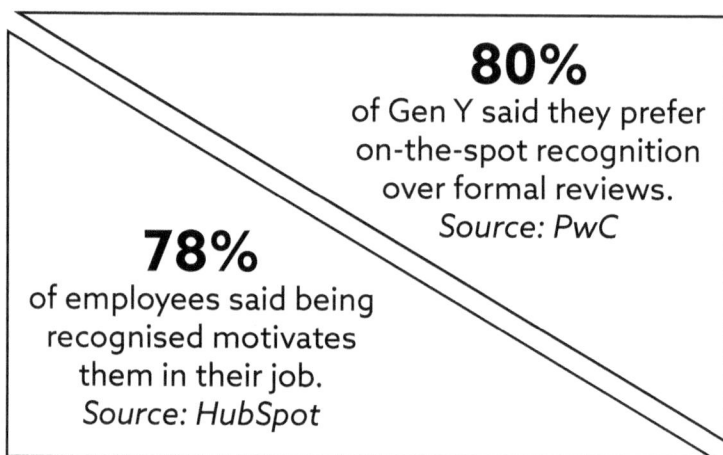

80%
of Gen Y said they prefer on-the-spot recognition over formal reviews.
Source: PwC

78%
of employees said being recognised motivates them in their job.
Source: HubSpot

... BECAUSE YOUR MANAGERS AREN'T SKILLED, CONFIDENT OR EMPOWERED:

""I had one member of my team who would schedule appointments when we were supposed to have the performance meeting. She dodged me all the time. I wasted so much time chasing."

"The paperwork is so time consuming. I don't know what happens to the information once I submit it. I'm told it is part of determining the

annual development plan for the organisation, but I rarely see anything on that plan from what my team asks for or what I ask for!"

"I dread these meetings. Sometimes the development part of the conversation is like trying to get blood from a stone. It's ridiculous because we both know the budget and time are rarely there, even if a program is offered. And don't get me started on the difficult conversations ... argh!"

"When we dropped the annual reviews, I was relieved, but we weren't given any direction, training or support for the 'in-the-moment' feedback."

Only
8%
of companies surveyed
believe their performance
management process is
highly effective in driving
business value.
Source: Saba

So many people struggle to initiate feedback because there is a lack of structure or a fear of how the receiver may react. Although these are two very real and fundamental blocks to feedback for anyone who is expected to have feedback conversations, using the structure – the formula – in this book will minimise any potential negative reaction.

The EECC (Example, Effect, Coach, Commit) formula explained in this book has been tested and proven to boost the feedback giver's confidence. This is because it provides a reliable process to follow, milestones to reach and insights to look out for that indicate when to move to the next step in the conversation. When feedback givers use EECC to plan their feedback, it also has a positive impact on the feedback receiver – they feel more valued, engaged and empowered to take ownership of the way forward, rather than just being told what to do.

Would this work for you?

- A culture of feedback and growth across your organisation or business.

- Your employees helping to grow the business through direct contribution and development, stepping up and speaking up.

- Your employee turn-over rate reduced and staff morale and job satisfaction scores increased.

- More effective succession planning, leading to vacated roles being filled faster with existing employees prepared to take on the new challenge.

- Your company, business or practice reputation improved, leading to increased competitive advantage and attracting higher calibre employees, stakeholders and clients.

- Your employees and managers proactively engaging in constant feedback conversations.

Well-facilitated feedback leads to:

- Improved performance across the organisation.
- Decreased turnover.
- A more productive, skilled and loyal workforce.
- A more cost-effective, informative and engaging performance-appraisal process.
- Increased trust, confidence and openness between managers and employees.

S SALLY FOLEY-LEWIS

CHAPTER 3

THE SECRETS TO FEEDBACK SUCCESS

3.1 YOU
3.2 SAFETY
3.3 ENVIRONMENT
3.4 THE FOLLOW UP

When we make progress and get better at something, it is inherently motivating. In order for people to make progress, they have to get feedback and information on how they're doing.
– Dan Pink

Before unpacking the feedback formula it's essential to know that any feedback conversation will either blow up in your face or blow you away depending on a few critical elements.

3.1 YOU

Actually, to be specific, it's your attitude! What goes through your mind when you're about to have a feedback conversation? Do any of these thoughts sound familiar to you:

Not this again! I'm sick of repeating myself. Why can't they just get it?

I'd better bring a box of tissues because this employee will put on the waterworks to stall and misdirect the conversation.

This one is like Teflon, nothing seems to stick!

When you think about the conversation you're about to have and your mind wanders to the negative, you set yourself up for a negative outcome. Your attitude going into the conversation affects the result.

Even if any one of the above statements might be true, shift your thinking towards a more productive and positive view. For example:

What do I need to do differently so this employee gets it and we can co-create a more effective action plan?

Although the waterworks have happened in the past, I am determined to wait and persist with this conversation because the performance is the issue and the employee needs to know that. I need to show the employee that this is not a personal attack, it's a performance conversation.

What questions do I need to ask so the employee can see they have a responsibility in this situation?

Changing your attitude to a more productive and positive standpoint is not about being naïvely optimistic, it's about being helpful and showing the employee they are valued.

Check your reasons for giving feedback.

DO NOT GIVE FEEDBACK IF ...	DO GIVE FEEDBACK IF ...
You need to make yourself feel or appear superior or powerful.	You are concerned for your employee and their performance.
You're in a bad mood.	You know you can guide, support, coach and mentor your employee's performance.
You want to reprimand, condemn or demoralise your employees.	You have a sense of obligation or responsibility to lead your team effectively.
You simply want to appease someone.	It will increase and improve performance and engagement.

3.2 SAFETY

Corrective feedback needs to be handled privately. Even the most successfully planned and executed feedback conversation should be conducted in private. There is no value in risking embarrassment or humiliation by discussing an employee's performance improvement requirements in front of the team, your colleagues or customers. In addition, you will not be seen as respectful, trustworthy or caring as a leader. No one wins when corrective feedback is given in public.

Praise may also not be something an employee wants to be handled publicly. Not everyone wants to be singled out, even if it's for something positive. Check with the employee first. A public display of team praise is usually more accepted, especially in Australia.

Psychological safety is where individuals and teams feel safe to take interpersonal risks. Employees feel they can be themselves without fear of negative consequences that may impact their status, job or image. If people are not engaged in feedback conversations, it is important you consider their psychological safety – are they being judged or is their perception of the situation causing them to hold back because of any potential backlash?

Productivity in the workplace requires employees – and leaders – to feel safe to be themselves and contribute without reprisal.

3.3 ENVIRONMENT

So many workplaces are open and noisy. This makes it a challenge to find a quiet and private space to have a feedback conversation. Don't let this be your excuse to avoid the conversation or to have it publicly. Coffee shops and cafes are also not ideal, as others can overhear you. While the idea of having a nice coffee out is great, the reason for the meeting is feedback, not coffee.

CASE STUDY: COFFEE SHOPS ARE FOR COFFEE

While waiting for my take-away coffee, I stood near a table where two people were sitting. After a few moments, I realised I could hear their conversation and, with a glance at their table, I could see their notes and an annual performance form. I could hear the manager telling the employee he needed to improve his program completion rate as he wasn't as fast or accurate as others in the team.

I was uncomfortable hearing this and, when my coffee was ready and I turned to leave, I inadvertently caught the eye of the employee, I got the impression from his body language and facial expression that he was not comfortable. He was hunched over, as if to reduce the volume of the conversation. This makes it harder to have an effective conversation as it redirects valuable energy that should be focused on the conversation, not on minimising the impact of the environment.

An office or small meeting room where the door can be closed, phone calls diverted and there are no interruptions means you create the right environment so you and the feedback receiver can focus on the essential conversation. By doing this, you let the employee know you respect them and are not out to embarrass them.

3.4 FOLLOW UP

While more will be said about following up later in this chapter, it's important to state now that one of the biggest killers of productivity and positive results from a feedback conversation is the lack of follow up.

So, follow up!

If you set times and dates in your calendar to follow up, check progress and give ongoing support, then stick to them. The leader who doesn't follow up sends the message that the employee is not worthy or valued. This results in limited, if any, action being implemented.

Helping your people be accountable is a key component of people productivity.

CASE STUDY: NO FOLLOW UP = NO ACTION

Some years, six months would pass before the Managing Director of the company visited the branch office. During his rare visits, he would be quite authoritarian in what he wanted his sales staff to do. He would draw diagrams on the white board, talk about targets and warn how the company would suffer if quality and sales diminished.

He would then have a closed-door meeting with the Office Manager to berate him for the sales team failing to achieve what he wanted it to achieve since his previous visit.

Once he finished drilling the sales team and Office Manager, he would travel back to head office and the team wouldn't hear from him for weeks, sometimes months. Not a peep. Most significantly, no one would hear from him about any of the directions and actions he commanded during his branch-office visit.

While everyone would prefer the Managing Director to be less aggressive and more engaging with his communication, the other critical reasons why no one would act on his commands were obvious:

- He didn't encourage or empower staff to own the actions he wanted them to take.

- He didn't encourage the sales team to set clear actions, let alone provide it with clear actions with deadlines.

- In his meeting with the Office Manager, he neglected to brief him about what he actually wanted done and what follow-up should happen.

- He didn't tell the sales team or Office Manager he would follow up with them.

- And he never followed up with them!

Even if the Managing Director's style stayed the same, he would probably get slightly better results – albeit through fear – if he did follow up with his sales team and Office Manager regularly.

When you follow up with your employees or team, you show them you value them. You let them know the work they are doing is important and you care about their performance. This contributes to employees being accountable for the changes or actions agreed upon during the feedback conversation.

Following up may only require a five-minute phone call or it may need a lengthier discussion. How long and by what method the follow up takes place are determined by what is agreed in the feedback conversation and what actions and results have occurred since the feedback.

Do not under-estimate the value of the follow-up. So many managers and leaders complain of being too busy to follow-up yet also complain that they are forever chasing work and employees. By making the follow-up just as important as every other aspect of the conversation, the impact on productivity (time management) would drastically improve and the frustration of chasing work would drastically reduce.

S SALLY FOLEY-LEWIS

CHAPTER 4

THE SKILLS

4.1 EMOTIONAL INTELLIGENCE
4.2 QUESTIONS
4.3 LISTENING
4.4 FLEXIBILITY
4.5 PROBLEM SOLVING

Validation is not the same as feedback.
– Sally Foley-Lewis

Aim to give and receive feedback so everyone participating in the conversation has a positive experience – even in the difficult corrective conversations.

It's much better for positive and productive working relationships when the feedback conversation focuses on the problem or behaviour, not the person. A solutions-focused attitude and approach work best.

There are key skills that help create successful feedback conversations:

4.1 EMOTIONAL INTELLIGENCE

Many great books have been written about emotional intelligence. I recommend that if you want to continually improve your leadership, influence and impact, then you should read *Emotional Intelligence: Why It Can Matter More Than IQ* by Daniel Goleman. Two other books that complement the improvement of emotional intelligence are *Mindset: How You Can Fulfil Your Potential* by Dr Carol S. Dweck and *Grit: The Power of Passion and Perseverance* by Angela Duckworth.

Emotional intelligence is about awareness, control and the expression of emotions. It's also about knowing how to behave towards and respond to others. In the context of feedback conversations, your emotional intelligence must keep your emotions in check while also ensuring you have empathy for the person receiving the feedback.

Your ability to keep your emotions in check means you can communicate from a position of objectivity and empathy. Recall the last time you were angry and blurted out something you later regretted. That's not keeping your emotions in check.

Keeping your emotions in check is not the same as not feeling frustrated, angry, disappointed, delighted or happy. It's about being aware of these emotions, understanding what they mean and not letting them drive the communication. Additionally, emotional intelligence includes identifying how the feedback receiver may feel and having empathy for them. Great feedback givers can pick up on the receiver's emotions and acknowledge – or validate – them.

Everyone – yes, you too – is entitled to their emotions. It's how they are handled that determines the success of the conversation.

4.2 ASKING QUALITY QUESTIONS

Asking quality questions goes hand in hand with gathering quality information. Ask questions that encourage the conversation to flow. These are generally open questions that start with *how* and *what*.

Examples of questions that encourage a conversation to flow:

- What specifically has been the biggest challenge to completing the task?
- How can you streamline the process?
- What short-term support do you need to complete the project?

The person who asks the question controls the conversation. This means you can direct the conversation with a question. It also means you will do less talking and more listening. I'll repeat that: you will do **less talking** and **more listening**!

Here are some tips for asking quality questions that result in greater engagement and results:

a) One Question at a Time

Ask only one question at a time. I'm sure you've observed or even been in a situation where one person has started to ask a question, then went on to explain why they were asking the question, then went on to give more background detail, then went on to practically answer the question, then went on, and on, and on …

While well intended, what happens is the real question is never properly asked and an answer is never properly provided.

Ask one question, then listen. Sounds simple, yet it's not always easy to do. It may take practice.

b) Silence is a Valuable Tool

Use silence. When a question is asked, sometimes the response is an immediate, "I don't know," or a period of silence. Avoid jumping in to fill the silence. Let the person think. Give them the space to reply. This shows the person you're prepared to wait for an answer. If you must speak, encourage the person to think about your question as if they did know the answer. Ask what their initial thoughts are.

A handout listing different types of questions and examples is included in the extra resources: go to: http://www.sallyfoleylewis. com/successful-feedback-extras/

4.3 LISTENING

Listening gives you clues as to what you can do to improve processes, systems and relationships.

When you listen carefully, you demonstrate respect and concern for the other person. This encourages that person to feel comfortable enough to contribute further to the conversation.

Listening allows you to detect possible reasons why performance has slipped or why mistakes have been made so you can guide the conversation to resolutions. It's not an opportunity to find out who is to blame and shame. Don't get caught in that vortex. If the receiver deflects responsibility, assure them it's not a matter of blame but an opportunity to learn and improve. If they persist in deflecting responsibility, use quality, probing questions to explore why. In essence, you park the topic of the feedback and explore the issue of responsibility.

A wonderful resource for helping you learn to listen deeply is *Deep Listening: Impact Beyond Words* by Oscar Trimboli.

4.4 FLEXIBILITY

Being flexible is about taking the conversation where it needs to go. Be prepared to go back to clarify earlier discussion points and to re-confirm an agreed action. If the actions discussed and initially agreed upon don't gain commitment, then don't persist. Find the right actions so the employee is willing to act on them.

Give yourself and the employee time to have an effective conversation without feeling rushed. This means productive and positive outcomes will be achieved sooner rather than later. If you simply follow the feedback structure in a linear fashion, get a weak commitment and don't go back to check which actions need changing for greater commitment, then you can expect a poor result later. Time spent in the feedback conversation ensuring the actions have gained a commitment from the employee will produce a long-term positive result. Flexibility now saves you time, money and sanity later.

4.5 PROBLEM SOLVING

It's important to find ways to help the person do their own problem solving. Avoid giving them the answers immediately. Even if you know the right answer, stop! Let the person think. Don't cave in to the pressure to speed through the conversation.

Problem-solving skills involve identifying what the real problem is and breaking it down into manageable chunks of single or smaller tasks. So often, we provide a solution rather than identify a problem and when that happens, we limit opportunities for the employee to provide their own solutions.

An example would be:

> **Solution disguised as a problem:**
> *We need more space in this office.*

Problem identification:
The workspace is cluttered and congested.

You may already understand the problem and how to solve it; however, better, longer-lasting results are achieved when you encourage the employee to work out and suggest actions for change. You can do this by asking quality questions that encourage the employee to think the problem through. If the employee struggles to think of potential solutions, then you can provide prompts or suggestions. If you must give suggestions, give three so the employee must choose. The aim is for the employee to have as much ownership of the actions as possible.

Emotional intelligence, asking quality questions, listening, flexibility and problem solving are the foundational skills for successful feedback conversations. Fine-tuning these skills will benefit you in more ways than just feedback conversations – they are skills for leadership and life.

SALLY FOLEY-LEWIS

CHAPTER 5

TYPES OF FEEDBACK RECEIVERS

Nothing we do is more important than hiring people. At the end of the day, you bet on people, not strategies.
– Lawrence Bossidy

You might have all sorts of colourful names for the challenging characters you've been required to have feedback conversations with, and giving them colourful descriptions might provide you with some short-term relief. Understanding feedback givers helps provide valuable guidance in how to handle the conversations. Obviously not all conversations will be the same and that's because people are different! While stereotyping can be quite negative, giving some thought to the different types of feedback receivers can be helpful for determining how to be the most effective feedback giver.

To improve the feedback conversations you conduct you do need to dig a bit deeper to understand why some people are really difficult to engage in a conversation while others are fantastic.

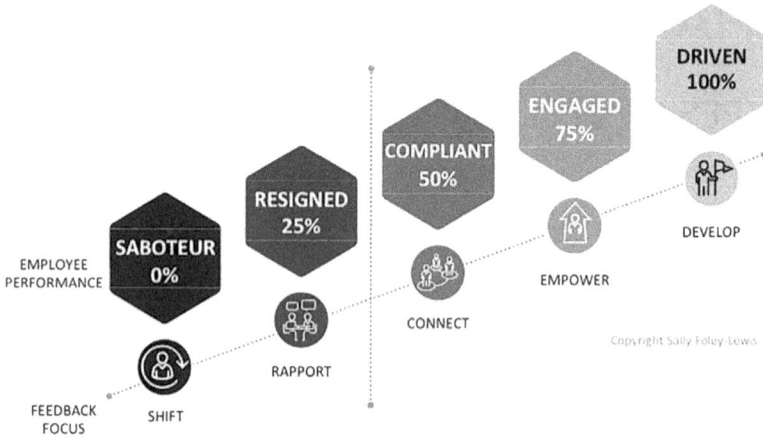

Copyright Sally Foley-Lewis

Saboteur

As the title says, the saboteur goes out of their way to avoid performance improvement and feedback conversations. Their performance might be below average to just on average, so they get away with some of their sabotaging behaviours. They also might conduct their sabotage in underhanded ways that aren't easily spotted, or they may draw in others so they can't be solely held responsible.

Examples of the saboteur include gossips; someone who undermines ideas, change processes and projects; and a person who congratulates someone who's been praised, then finds a way to spoil the moment for that person.

The focus of this feedback conversation is *shift*. This person needs to dramatically shift their attitude and performance in one of two directions: improve or be removed!

Resigned

A resigned feedback receiver is one who shows up but has "checked out". For any number of reasons, this employee is struggling. For example:

- They're bored.
- Their values and the organisation's values are misaligned.
- They feel as though nothing they do is enough.
- They have another job lined up.
- Trust is missing.
- They don't feel as though they are growing in the role.
- They know or perceive changes, such as job cuts, are coming soon.

The focus for this employee in any general or feedback conversation is *rapport*. When you have a rapport with this employee, you have more trust and, therefore, more likelihood of finding out what's going on, which leads to being able to plan for improvements.

Compliant

Going along to get along! The compliant feedback receiver will say exactly what they think you want to hear. And if you don't pick up on that straight away, you'll find yourself back in another feedback conversation much sooner than you anticipated, simply because nothing or very little has progressed.

The focus for the compliant feedback receiver is to explore and *connect* with what they want to do. This means asking them what they want, then being silent to give them time to consider their answer. Be careful not to jump in and speak before they've answered. Get comfortable with silence.

Engaged

The engaged feedback receiver is attentive and keen. The risk with the engaged employee is that it's easy to ignore them, as they seem to be doing well. It's usually those who struggle or who have dropped in their performance who get the lion's share of the leader's attention.

Your focus with the engaged employee should be on *empowering* them to contribute, share ideas, speak up and take a seat at the table. It's about leveraging their energy to boost results.

Driven

The driven feedback receiver is like the engaged employee in that they may not receive as much attention as poorer performing staff. However, the driven employee has energy that needs to be directed towards their development.

Developing the driven employee serves to support any leader's succession plan. This employee is the one you should prepare to step into your role when you go on leave or move on in your career.

CHAPTER 6

THE EECC FORMULA

6.1 THE THREE ABILITIES
6.2 GIVING PRAISE WITH EECC
6.3 GIVING CORRECTIVE FEEDBACK WITH EECC
6.4 POINTS TO AVOID WITH PRAISE AND
CORRECTIVE FEEDBACK
6.5 FEEDBACK EXAMPLES BASED ON REAL
CASE STUDIES
6.6 USE ALL THE EECC FORMULA

Criticism, like rain, should be gentle enough to nourish a man's growth without destroying his roots.
– Frank A. Clark

The threes As of awareness, action and achievement were discussed in Chapter 1. As you look over the feedback structure below, you can see more specifically how they fit and how fundamental they are to any feedback conversation.

The diagram shows the essential elements of the feedback conversation – the EECC feedback formula!

Note that while there is some logic to structuring your conversation from left to right, i.e. example, effect, coach, then commit, you may find that you may need to flex back to previous steps to ensure the feedback receiver has full awareness of the situation and is designing actions or action plans they will commit to.

6.1 THE THREE ABILITIES

Just as you are aiming for awareness, action and achievement as a result of the feedback conversation, you can use the three abilities to check in on progress during the conversation.

Responsibility

If the feedback receiver has understood the situation and the impact it is having on themselves, the team, the work and results, they will take responsibility for their actions.

Sometimes, simply explaining what you have seen will be enough for the person to understand the example and effect. Other times, it may take a little more effort on your part to link the person to the effect, especially if they are saboteurs or resigned. This is where having specific examples are essential, as you'll discover later in this chapter.

You may want to experiment with either describing the effect or asking the feedback giver if they can see or think of the possible impact/effect their performance has on others, the work, the bottom line and even their job security. Be careful – this is not about threatening them, it's about increasing their awareness and sense of responsibility so they can shift into action and change-ability.

Changeability

When the feedback receiver has understood the effect and you can tell they have ownership of the issue, coaching them through actions can be a smooth and simple process. This means the person is changeable.

When employees are new, resigned or have been given a project beyond their workload, capacity or skills, you may need to use more questions and listening to guide them. As a last resort, provide action options the employee can choose from.

Accountability

Accountability is like having a valuer show up and placing a value far greater than you anticipated on your efforts. When people are accountable, distractions are significantly minimised. This is because the value of the work is far greater and has more importance placed on it. There's no point having a feedback conversation if you don't follow up and people don't act. Accountability is the linchpin of action and achievement.

6.2 GIVING PRAISE WITH EECC

Example:

- Provide a specific example of the person's good work so they can clearly link their actions to the feedback.
- Be specific. Thank them. The more specific you are, the better the person can understand and appreciate their own positive or helpful behaviour.

Effect:

- Provide the person with insight into the benefits (effects) of their actions.
- Explain the effect of the person's behaviour. This means you must answer any questions the person has about why you are highlighting their behaviour. You are answering the person's "so what?"
- Describe the benefits to the individual, team, organisation, budget, profits, reputation, etc.

Coach:

- Facilitate (not direct or dictate) a discussion about how the person's actions can be continued, shared with or taught to others, or applied in other areas.
- Encourage the person to implement an action plan.
- If no further action is needed or can be taken, simply (yet importantly) thank the person for their efforts.

Commit:

- Establish a commitment to embed actions for future results and success.
- Ensure commitment by:
    - Setting and sticking to follow-up dates.
    - Asking the employee how they would like you to help them be accountable.
    - Encourage them to offer other ideas.
    - Re-state your gratitude for their performance.

Not everyone likes to be praised or acknowledged in public, so be mindful of how the person would prefer to be praised. Give praise as soon as possible after the event.

See Section 6.5 for examples of this conversation structure.

Action

Awareness

Achievement

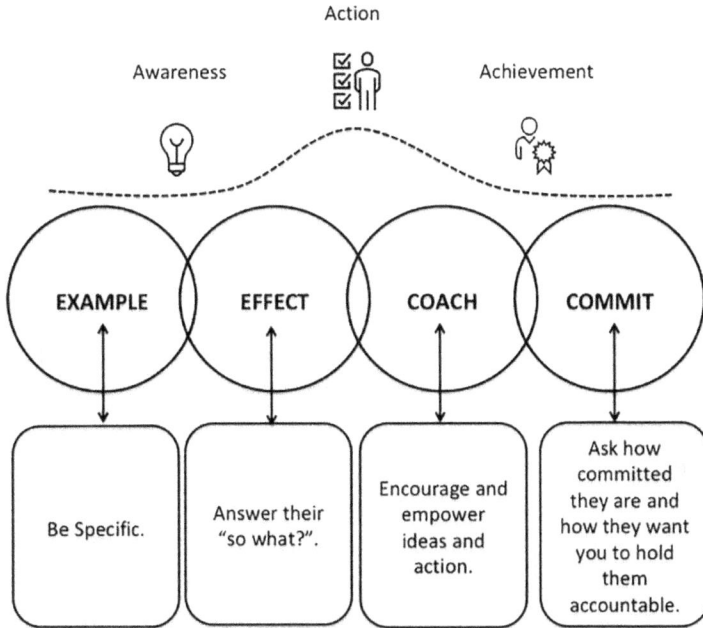

EXAMPLE	EFFECT	COACH	COMMIT
Be Specific.	Answer their "so what?".	Encourage and empower ideas and action.	Ask how committed they are and how they want you to hold them accountable.

6.3 GIVING CORRECTIVE FEEDBACK WITH EECC

Example:

- Provide a specific example of the negative, incorrect or damaging behaviour/s or action/s so the person can clearly recall and link to what you're saying.
- The more specific you are, the better the person can connect with the situation.

Effect:

- Give a clear explanation of the effect of the person's behaviour, such as the impact it has on the team, organisation, budget, safety, project success, future opportunities, etc.
- This will give the person a reason as to why their behaviour was incorrect. Explaining the effect answers their "so what?"

Note: There may be valid reasons for the behaviour that need to be addressed. These reasons could include the person not knowing the proper process, not being kept up to date on procedural changes or not having the skills to do the task.

The amount of time these reasons have impacted the work will also need to be addressed. Focus the discussion on understanding when the problem or behaviour occurred. You may need to reassure the person that the questions are about understanding the core problem, not about assigning blame. When you blame, you create a roadblock to overcoming the issue because people become defensive. It's also important you discourage the employee from blaming others.

Coach:

- Facilitate (not direct or dictate) the discussion about what changes the employee can make.
- Listen and use quality questions to coach the employee to identify actions for change. (Remember to check the extra resources available: http://www.sallyfoleylewis.com/ successful-feedback-extras/)

- The more the employee is engaged, empowered and enthused to identify these actions, the greater they will own the process – and the more likely that positive changes will occur.

Commit:

- Establish a commitment to embed the actions for results and success.
- You can address commitment in two ways:
  1. Them: Close the conversation by getting the person to commit to the new behaviour.
  2. You: Assure them you are committed to helping them. Ask them how they would like you to support them and keep them accountable.
- Set follow-up dates and times and stick to them!

Corrective feedback is valuable only when it is clearly understood, when actions for change are identified and when there is commitment.

See Section 6.5 for examples of this conversation structure.

Remember, if you don't address poor performance or mistakes as soon as possible, the negative impact on productivity, resources, relationships and finances will be prolonged.

Once corrective feedback is dealt with and performance is back to the right standard, avoid focusing on it or reminding the person about it. Let it go. At the time of an annual performance review, it would be a positive gesture to praise the extra effort the person has made to get their performance back to the right standard.

If the performance does not improve, you may need to escalate the issue to a disciplinary process or a performance-management process. Be sure to follow your organisation's policies for this. If you need some assistance, please do reach out: sally@sallyfoleylewis.com.

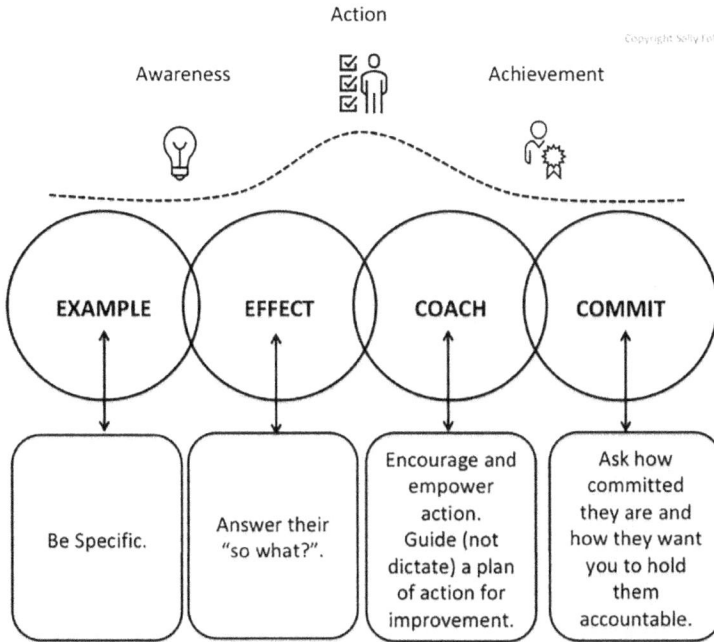

6.4 POINTS TO AVOID WITH PRAISE AND CORRECTIVE FEEDBACK

Avoid insincere, vague and irrelevant feedback. Statements such as "great job" without a reference to the task will not provide enough of a direct link for the employee to know exactly what they did well.

Praise boosts the ego and nurtures confidence. Who doesn't want that? You don't need to go overboard. Be specific and show you sincerely value the work they have done.

Be mindful that you are fair to all when it comes to giving praise. If others see you praising only one or two people repeatedly, it can be seen as favouritism, which impacts those you praise, the productivity of the team and the relationship between you and your team.

Some leaders believe giving praise diminishes their power or authority. They are quick to criticise and never give praise. The working relationships in these environments are often strained, with employees feeling uneasy at their work. This impacts productivity as staff do the minimum amount of work possible. They expend their energy avoiding criticism rather than on more positive and productive pursuits, such as bringing innovation and creativity to their work.

Avoid letting your ego get in the way of genuinely positive, open and honest working relationships. This is not about getting deeply personal or making everyone your best friend. It is about building relationships so your people feel safe to try new things without constant criticism.

6.5 FEEDBACK EXAMPLES BASED ON REAL CASE STUDIES

Praise Example No. 1:

EXAMPLE I want to take a minute to discuss how pleased I am that you took the initiative to review and streamline the job-sheet process.

EFFECT   Since you did that, I've noticed a much quicker turnaround in reporting the completions to the customer relations department. I'm also tracking to see if there have been other savings, such as actual job completion times.

COACH   You've got great initiative. Is there any other area you are keen to review or is there anything else in the job-sheet process you think can be further developed?

Allow discussion: ask quality questions and listen. Coach the employee to create an action plan, if relevant.

COMMIT   I want to close our conversation by again saying thank you and letting you know I'm committed to supporting you with the next project. I want to check how committed you are to keep going.

Have you created an action plan that excites you?

How can I help you stay accountable to this plan?

Leave the conversation on a good note. Encourage the person to have the last say about the feedback, such as how they feel about the next steps discussed during the coach step.

Praise Example No. 2:

EXAMPLE   You did a brilliant job of getting the project finished ahead of schedule, particularly driving the team while keeping morale up and costs down.

EFFECT   This has given us a 10% buffer in the budget and almost three months' wiggle room on the other two projects. I can tell you the rest of the team will be mightily impressed!

   The board has also been made aware and is looking for a way to recognise you for what you've done. Are you okay with some public acknowledgment and recognition?

COACH   I'm keen to know your thoughts on what you did in the project that could be done on other project sites.

   Allow discussion: ask quality questions and listen. Coach the employee to create an action plan, if relevant.

   Is this something you would like to continue with? How would that look like for you operationally?

COMMIT   I want to close our conversation by again saying thank you. I really am very pleased and thank you for all your effort. Lastly, please rest assured that I'll support you in the implementation.

Now, can I check how committed you are to seeing this continue?

How can I help you stay accountable to this plan?

Leave the conversation on a good note. Encourage the person to have the last say about the feedback, such as how they feel about the next steps discussed during the coach step.

Praise Example No. 3:

EXAMPLE The sales figures are in and you had a brilliant month, thank you. I noticed in your plan you had set a 5% increase yet pulled in 9.75%. Well done! You must be pleased with yourself, as you should be.

EFFECT This is an awesome result and will give the team a real motivational boost. Given we are also talking about how tough the market and economy are, this will show the team that exceeding expectations can be done.

COACH What was it about your approach or your efforts that made the difference this month?

Allow discussion: aim to learn about possible strategies that can be replicated or shared across other areas and/or with other staff. Ask quality questions and listen.

Would you be keen to share some of these actions with the team?

Or

How can we share these actions or tips with the rest of the team?

Or

How can these results be continued?

Allow discussion: ask quality questions and listen. Coach the employee to create an action plan, if relevant.

COMMIT Again, thank you for your good work and great sales figures. Let me know how I can help you keep this up. I want you to have the support you need.

Note: Leave the conversation on a good note. Encourage the person to have the last say about the feedback, such as how they feel about the next steps discussed during the coach step.

THANK YOU NOTES: PRAISE

Whenever someone has been generous with their time and wisdom for my benefit, I send them a thank you note.

Some may call it a strategy. I call it good manners. It costs me very little to send a note of thanks. And sometimes I get a message back, such as, "Oh thank you so much, I didn't expect that. So nice to get something handwritten, something personal."

Corrective Feedback Example No. 1:

EXAMPLE   I want to bring to your attention the required weekly work (specifically state what the work is) for XYZ client and ABC client. It hasn't been completed for the past three weeks.

Be specific so the person can make the link.

EFFECT   By not completing the weekly work, we cannot achieve the results for our clients, which they expect and pay us for. When the work is not done, the client has a right to not pay us and that directly impacts our cash flow, profits and ability to operate.

What has happened in the past three weeks that has caused the work to not be completed?

Allow discussion: ask quality questions and listen.

CHANGE   What can you do to turn this situation around?

Or

You can appreciate this work needs to be done regularly. Our clients directly rely on regular input. What actions can you take today to catch up?

Or

How can you fix the problem and move this forward so the work can be done weekly and not fall behind?

Allow discussion: ask quality questions and listen.

Coach the employee to create a plan of action with the person. Encourage the person to develop action steps so they have complete ownership of the plan.

COMMIT   I want to close our conversation by encouraging you to get on top of this work. I think you've got a good plan now to get back up to speed. I'm committed to supporting you with this, so please come to me if there are any hiccups along the way.

How committed are you to getting on with this work now?

How would you like me to help you stay accountable for these new actions?

Leave the conversation on a good note. Encourage the person to have the last say about the feedback, such as how committed they feel about the next steps discussed during the coach step.

Corrective Feedback Example No. 2:

EXAMPLE   I want to bring to your attention your late arrival to work recently. I've noticed you arrived at 9.15am last Monday, 9.20am on Tuesday, 9.45am on Thursday and today at 9.20am.

Be specific so the person can make the link.

Vague examples such as "late this week" will not provide a strong enough reference point for the employee. The more specific the example, the better the employee will be to connect with the behaviour. There will also be less chance of the employee finding flimsy excuses or brushing the feedback off because there isn't enough evidence.

EFFECT   I'm not sure if you're aware of the impact your late arrivals have had on others. For example, one staff member needed to reschedule a client meeting because they couldn't leave the office unattended. While it's not life and death, it does impact our client relationships. We don't want to mess clients about or lose clients. I also wanted to chat with you on Tuesday morning about Mr Smith's account before I met with him and you weren't here for me to do that. I wanted to get as much information about the account as possible. With you not here, I wasn't fully prepared. This left me concerned that our company didn't look professional.

What are your thoughts on the impact of being late?

Allow discussion: ask quality questions and listen.

There may be valid reasons that need to be addressed. Focus the discussion on understanding the underlying reason why the person has been late. Avoid any direct blame.

Are you aware of the policy about hours of work and lateness?

If necessary, explain the policy or remind them of it.

COACH   What do you need to do to arrive on time or cover the time you miss by being late?

Or

How can you turn this situation around?

Encourage the person to problem solve rather than you direct them. Ask quality questions and listen.

Coach the employee to create a plan of action with the person. Encourage them to develop the action steps so they have complete ownership of the plan.

COMMIT   Thank you for being open and honest about the situation. I know you are normally attentive with your timing, so I want you to know I am here to support you as best I can. How committed are you to turning this around?

How would you like me to help you stay accountable for these new actions?

Leave the conversation on a good note. Encourage the person to have the last say about the feedback, such as how committed they feel about the next steps discussed during the coach step.

Corrective Feedback Example No. 3:

EXAMPLE   I want to have a chat with you about the monthly reports you've been submitting. You may have noticed that for the past four months, the reports have been returned to you with many more corrections required. (Have copies on hand and show the employee.) We all make mistakes. I'm just noticing a bit of a difference in quality these past few months.

EFFECT   Because of the extra time needed to make the corrections, the reporting is being held up at the GM's office, which gives his office less time to prepare their reports for the board. There is a clear knock-on effect.

Prior to these past four months, everything was fine. What has happened to impact the quality of the reports lately?

Allow discussion: ask quality questions and listen.

There may be valid reasons beyond the control of the employee, which need to be addressed. Focus the discussion on understanding the underlying reason why the person's work standard has slipped. Avoid direct blame.

COACH   What help do you need to get the reports back to standard?

Or

What other work can you delegate, even temporarily, so you can catch up?

Allow discussion by encouraging the employee to problem solve. Ask quality questions and listen.

Coach the employ to create a plan of action with the person. Encourage them to develop the action steps so they have ownership of the plan

COMMIT   I'm glad we talked about this. Your work is normally really good and I wanted to make sure everything was okay with you. Thank you for helping problem solve this and finding a way forward. I am here to support you as best I can. Out of a score of 10 (10 being the most), how committed are you to putting this plan into action?

How can I help you stay accountable for these new actions?

Leave the conversation on a good note. Encourage the person to have the last say about the feedback, such as how committed they feel about the next steps discussed during the coach step.

6.6 USE ALL THE EECC FORMULA

For Praise:

The EECC formula is as flexible as you want to make it, however, be sure to use all parts of the formula for a successful outcome.

- If you skip giving a specific **EXAMPLE**, the foundational understanding of the feedback may be lost or misunderstood.
- If you skip explaining the **EFFECT** of the behaviour, the value of the praise may be understated.
- If you skip the opportunity to encourage the person to suggest options or value-added ideas in the **COACH** stage, you may miss enhanced productivity, opportunities or greater results in the future.
- If you skip securing their **COMMITMENT**, you fail to achieve accountability (yours and theirs).

For Corrective Feedback:

Treat the EECC formula as a flexible tool to keep the conversation focused and objective. Be sure to use all parts of the formula for a successful outcome.

- If you miss giving a specific **EXAMPLE**, the foundational understanding of the problem may not make sense.
- If you skip explaining the **EFFECT** of the employee's behaviour, the importance of the feedback will be lost or underestimated.

- If you neglect to encourage and **COACH** the employee to identify and plan actions for improved performance, you and the employee miss development opportunities in terms of problem solving, goal setting and planning. Most importantly, both parties will miss a positive outcome.
- If you skip securing their **COMMITMENT**, you fail to achieve accountability (yours and theirs).

SALLY FOLEY-LEWIS

CHAPTER 7

RECEIVING FEEDBACK

7.1 POINTS TO CONSIDER WHEN RECEIVING FEEDBACK
7.2 USING THE EECC FORMULA TO RECEIVE FEEDBACK
7.3 USE ALL THE EECC FORMULA

> *Being entirely honest with oneself is a good exercise.*
> – Sigmund Freud

Just as it is your role to provide feedback, you also need to be able to receive it. Your own productivity can improve by asking for and receiving feedback. Feedback from your employees, peers and senior leaders is invaluable for gaining greater insights into your leadership, behaviours, interpersonal communication, influence and impact.

When asking your employees or direct reports for feedback, it must be done with an assurance that they are safe to provide the feedback.

The more specific your questions, the better feedback you'll get. This is where the EECC formula helps create a safe framework for others to provide feedback:

- If you don't connect with the feedback, ask for an EXAMPLE. Try something like this:

  Thank you for pointing this out. So I understand this a little better, have you got a specific example of [the behaviour, the piece of work, the situation]?

- If you don't understand the importance or impact of their feedback, ask for clarity on the EFFECT. Try something like this:

  I'm not sure I understand the degree of importance or severity of this issue. What effect/impact did [the behaviour, piece of work, situation] have on the [outcome, deadline, team, budget]?

- If you are unsure how to make changes, ask for some COACHING to set goals and create an action plan. Try something like this:

  Thank you for the feedback you've given me. I'm not sure where to start to make changes, so I would greatly appreciate your help in coaching me/guiding me to create an action plan

- If you want help to stay accountable, ask for it through COMMITMENT. Try something like this:

  I appreciate the time you've spent giving me this feedback. I am committed to making the changes/implementing this new action plan. Can I please meet with you next week to check progress? [Schedule the meeting before you finish the conversation.]

This is explained further in 7.2 Using the EECC Formula to Receive Feedback.

The following questions will help you decide whether it's appropriate for you to ask for feedback. Ask yourself:

1. When was the last time I had a review of my work and my level of productivity?

2. I don't know what is expected of this task or project. What are the success factors? What's the timeline, budget, support, etc.?

3. Was a specific task or project not completed well?

4. How can I work out the cause of the problems with a project or task?

5. Someone else got a promotion I applied for. I was equally suited for the role. What have I missed or need to do to get the same promotional opportunity?

6. I did a fantastic job completing the task/project and I would like help to identify how to take it further. How do I determine if this success can be replicated elsewhere? Or: How can I replicate the success in other areas?

7. What's happening to my role and what opportunities are available to me given recent changes in our workplace/industry?

8. I want to stay with this company, yet this role is not right for me. What skills do I need to develop or improve to be considered for other roles?

9. I can't stand working with my colleague – he speaks to me and treats me like a subordinate. How do I deal with him?

10. I think I run a tight ship but the staff satisfaction survey results are low. Productivity seems okay, but staff turnover is creeping up. What can I do to address these issues?

If any of these questions even slightly relate to you, ask for feedback.

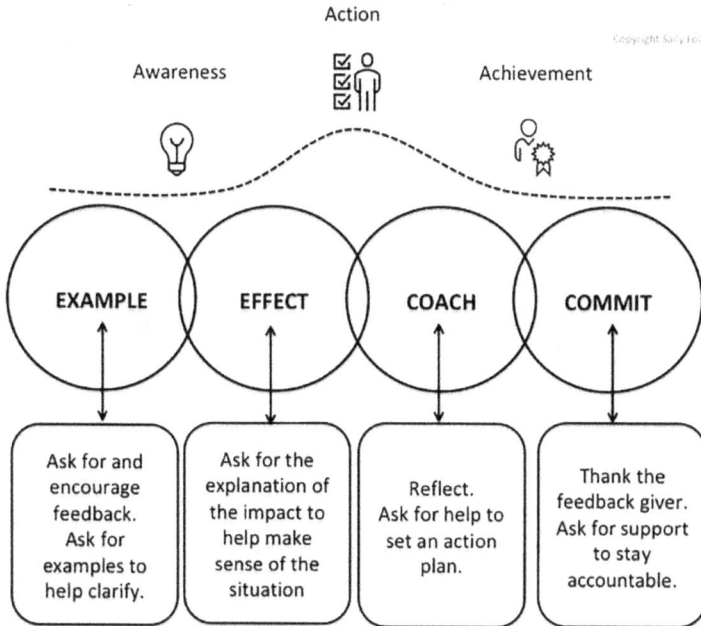

7.1 POINTS TO CONSIDER WHEN RECEIVING FEEDBACK

As you receive feedback, it's important to keep in mind that:

- Not everyone finds it easy to give feedback.
- Not everyone knows how to give feedback properly.
- Feedback can be subjective, so evaluate it objectively.
- There is always some learning or insight to be gained from feedback that is meant to help you, not hinder you, so seek it.
- Most of the time, people have good intentions, so be gracious when they give you feedback.

Be considerate of the feedback giver's time and priorities. Turning up at their office or desk unexpectedly and expecting them to give you quality feedback is inconsiderate. Schedule some time and help the feedback giver prepare for the conversation. If you want feedback on specific tasks, actions or projects, let the feedback giver know so they can reflect on your performance and prepare. Ask specific questions.

Share the *Successful Feedback* book with them or buy them a copy as a thoughtful contribution to their professional development.

Things to avoid:

If feedback is not delivered well, avoid:

* Jumping to conclusions.
* Being defensive.
* Reacting harshly or negatively, even if the feedback giver is being harsh, aggressive or negative.

If you feel you are being attacked or you both need to calm down, ask for a 5 to 10-minute break. This will give both of you time to regroup. Re-start the feedback conversation by focusing on the behaviour or developing an action plan to move forward. Remember to keep it professional, performance-focused and not personal.

IMPORTANT

When you lead a feedback conversation, you want the employee to be engaged and actively, if not proactively, work towards positive outcomes. Your boss will have the same objective for you. Asking for help to do this is not a weakness – it's a strength. It demonstrates a desire to improve yourself, the processes and profits.

Reassurance:

Seeking relevant, valid and helpful feedback for improved performance is one thing. Seeking constant (and time-consuming) reassurance is another. Make sure you know the difference. Ask for feedback but also take the initiative to reflect on your own performance to work out for yourself what you can do to improve. If you would like some reassurance, it's worth reflecting on why you feel you need it. Ask yourself what information or support is missing that triggers your desire for greater reassurance. Once you have some clarity on what you need, you can be more specific in your request for help.

If you take the time to source feedback, which also means utilising another person's time, then listen. Pay attention to what they say. Avoid reacting. Avoid interrupting. Just listen.

CASE STUDY: ENGAGING THE EMPLOYEE IN THE PROBLEM-SOLVING PROCESS

When I landed in my first project management role, I quickly found myself fielding all manner of questions. I was required to constantly problem solve for others. I admit, I often thought, "These are smart people – why aren't they thinking for themselves?"

So I decided to turn the conversation around, whenever I was presented with a problem from a direct report I asked them what they thought; what they'd like to do; what research they had done into the issue.

Some people would cut the conversation short so they could do some more self-directed work on the problem; others were in need of more direction. I continued with questions that lead to them devising a plan to move forward.

I soon worked out that some people really enjoyed the opportunity to find their own way forward, or offer up ideas, while others did need support to find the solutions to their problems. It helped me to find out who really needed help, who needed to be engaged more, and who simply became dependent on my role to do all the thinking for them.

I wanted people to take back, own and demonstrate their power of thinking, problem solving, showing their initiative and creativity, not so I didn't have to help, but so I could work out how I could help.

7.2 USING THE EECC FORMULA TO RECEIVE FEEDBACK

Example:

Be open, encouraging and ask for feedback. Not everyone will know you want feedback. Even in organisations where feedback is part of a formal annual review process, the feedback may be limited to simply completing the mandatory paperwork, which means the feedback giver can avoid conversations of substance.

By asking for feedback, you also let the feedback giver know you:

- Want to know what they think of your performance.
- Want to work to standards and expectations.
- Are prepared to learn, develop and improve.

If the feedback giver seems reticent to provide feedback, ask specific, quality questions that help open the conversation. Vague questions can lead to vague answers. It might be easier to start with a specific question that relates to one direct aspect of your role. For example:

Avoid vague questions like:

What do you think of my performance over the past six months?

Instead, ask more specific, helpful questions like:

I'd like some feedback on my performance. Specifically, in relation to managing the XYZ project. What's one positive aspect and one aspect for improvement I could take forward as I complete the project?

Ask for specific examples if you're not sure what the feedback relates to. Use quality questions to get more details and examples that will help you understand what the feedback giver is saying.

In summary:

- Be encouraging and seek feedback.
- Ask for examples to help make sense of the feedback.
- Be positive about the process and the person giving the feedback.
- Listen to what the person says – and listen some more!

Effect:

As the person provides feedback, it's important you understand what they are talking about so you can move forward and make any relevant changes. If you are not clear about what the person is referring to, ask what the effect or impact has been. For example:

What's been the impact of my behaviour on other team members, the success (or failure) of a project, quality or timeliness of work, wastage, etc.?

You may experience some feedback examples and effects as quite negative. Keep in mind this might be a challenging situation for the feedback giver, too, so avoid being defensive and blaming others.

Keep calm so you avoid using defensive or argumentative clarification questions, such as:

- What do you mean?
- When did I do that?
- Prove it!

Asking these questions in a defensive or argumentative tone creates further roadblocks to a quality conversation, which can negatively impact the working relationship.

Yes, it seems obvious to ask for clarification in a mature, calm manner. However, it's easy to quickly become defensive when the feedback giver is not constructive with their feedback.

Take the time to determine what helps you stay calm in stressful situations. For example, keep your breathing slow and calm and avoid interrupting the feedback giver, as this may cause the conversation to escalate into negative territory.

In summary:

- Ask the feedback giver to explain the effect of the behaviour to help clarify the feedback.
- Stay calm.
- Avoid being defensive.

Change:

If you disagree with the feedback, determine whether you need to state your disagreement. It might not be necessary to say anything other than thanking the person for their time. If you do think it is necessary or have been asked whether you agree or not, do so without attacking, making excuses or getting personal. Stay focused on the action or behaviour.

If you know why a situation occurred, calmly explain what happened. There may be a valid and reasonable explanation for why something occurred the way it did and the feedback giver may not have all the information at hand. Share your information with them, particularly with a view to brainstorming ideas for how to avoid negative situations reoccurring in the future, or how to replicate the positives in other aspects of your work or in the organisation.

Remain in the feedback conversation until agreeable solutions are developed. Ask for help to develop an action plan or ideas you can own and implement that will lead to the right standard of performance.

As you reflect on the conversation you've had, decide what and how to implement the ideas that have emerged from the feedback. Add these to your action plan. Be sure to work on the changes you've agreed upon.

In summary:

• Reflect on the feedback.
• It's okay to disagree. Do it with dignity.
• Ask for help to develop actions for change.

Commitment:

You've heard it before, "actions speak louder than words". Thanking the feedback giver is important but it may not mean much to them (and to the rest of the team or organisation) if you don't do anything with the feedback you've been given.

Make a commitment and demonstrate you have paid attention by implementing the actions you discussed and agreed upon.

As you implement the changes, follow up with the feedback giver on the actions you've taken. Encourage their continued support to help keep you accountable to the changes.

In summary:

- Be committed to making positive changes.
- Thank the feedback giver with words and actions.

7.3 USE ALL THE EECC FORMULA

Whether you or someone else initiates the conversation to receive feedback, be an active participant in the conversation so you are confident all aspects of the EECC formula are covered.

- If you don't ask for **EXAMPLES**, you may not fully understand the feedback.
- If you don't ask the feedback giver to explain the **EFFECT** of your behaviour, the foundational understanding and impact of the feedback may be lost.

- If you leave the conversation without looking for ways to improve you may miss opportunities for personal and professional development, having your feedback giver **COACH** you helps you devise the right action plan.
- If you skip assuring your **COMMITMENT**, you miss the opportunity to prove to others you can improve (especially to those who can influence your career prospects).

FEEDBACK CONVERSATION PLANNING TEMPLATE

The following is a template for you to plan out and use as a quick guide for your feedback conversations.

To get an A4 size copy plus feedback posters for your office go to http://www.sallyfoleylewis.com/successful-feedback-extras/

The template is for your personal use in feedback conversation NOT TO BE SOLD.

FEEDBACK CONVERSATION PLAN

☐ PRAISE   ☐ CORRECTIVE FEEDBACK

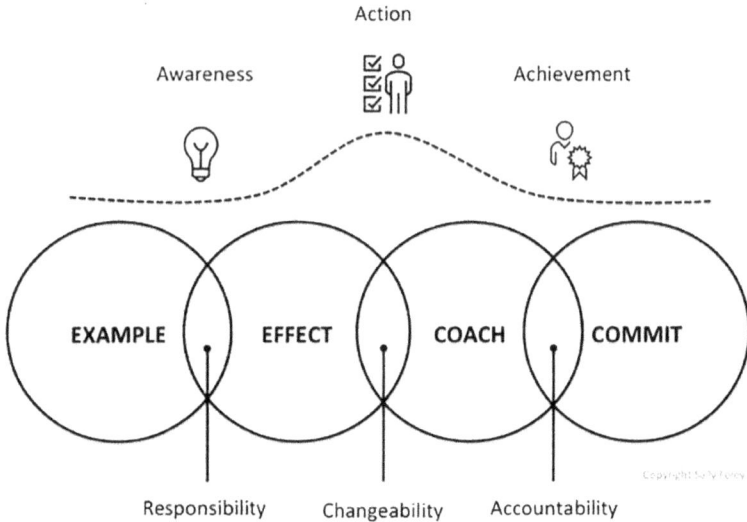

Action

Awareness   Achievement

EXAMPLE   EFFECT   COACH   COMMIT

Responsibility   Changeability   Accountability

EXAMPLE

Be specific: What, when, where, who …

_____

_____

_____

_____

EFFECT

How did this impact the team, the work, a deadline, a decision, the employee's job security ...

COACH

Write three questions that will prompt the person to think about the necessary options or actions:

1. _____

_____

2. _____

_____

3. _____

_____

Write three actions you can suggest as a last resort.

1. _____

   _____

2. _____

   _____

3. _____

   _____

COMMIT

Remember to ask how committed the person is to working the plan.

If they aren't sure, ask what other action they could implement or what it would take for them to be committed.

Ask the person how they would like you to help them stay accountable.

_____

_____

_____

_____

CHAPTER 8

FORMAL PERFORMANCE REVIEWS

*I believe in accessibility. I believe in honesty and a culture
that supports that. And you can't have that if you're not open to
receiving feedback.*
– Mindy Grossman

The EECC feedback formula works well within any formal performance review process, which, for many organisations, includes
the completing and submitting of forms, such as development
plans, progress reports and targets for bonuses.

The organisation's formal performance review process is often
met with dread or seen as an inconvenience that pops up once
or twice throughout the year. Many processes are so standardised
that the documentation doesn't always align with all the different
staff within an organisation. This usually comes about because the
logic was to create a streamlined process that would lead to cost
efficiencies. However, it ends up being a contributor to increased
costs.

CASE STUDY: I'M A TECHNICIAN, NOT AN ADMINISTRATION OFFICER

When my client first approached me, they had experienced their third year in a row of decreasing staff satisfaction and morale. Each year for three years, their surveys returned increasingly worse scores.

Part of the reason for this was the company's poor performance review process:

- It was process-led and not human focused.
- Managers were not trained in how to have quality feedback and development conversations.
- No informal regular feedback was given, only a formal meeting once or twice per year.
- The completion of paperwork was more important than anything written on the paperwork.
- The forms were not customised for different roles – everyone had the same form no matter if they were a technician, shift supervisor, administration manager or in-house counsel.

A search on popular recruitment sites for this company showed alarming reviews from past employees:

"The job was great but the management, culture, support, paperwork was soul destroying. Couldn't get out of there fast enough!"

If you identify with any element of this case study, consider:

1. Reviewing your entire performance review process, if you have the delegated authority to make improvements. If you need assistance with this, please reach out: sally@sallyfoleylewis.com.

2. Approaching a new way of giving feedback to your direct reports:

   - Have more informal feedback conversations throughout the year.
   - During the formal performance review meetings, put the human first and paperwork second. See these meetings as opportunities to:

     - Learn more about your team members, colleagues and boss.
     - Learn how the other person is coping with their workload, what they are achieving easily and what they struggle with.
     - Develop your own skills and the skills of the other person.
     - Build stronger working relationships.

All feedback conversations should be two-way, open and honest to help individuals aim to perform to the best of their ability. The paperwork for the formal review should merely support the conversation.

Different organisations have different processes for conducting their performance reviews. For example, both the feedback giver and receiver complete forms reviewing the performance of the previous period, then come together to discuss and compare results to inform a development plan. The EECC formula will help the conversation as:

- The **EXAMPLES** can be discussed in detail.
- The **EFFECT** of the behaviour or actions can be explained.
- **COACHING** will directly support the development of a new action plan and objectives for the next period.
- You can both assure **COMMITMENT** to the new actions being implemented.

The formal performance review meeting can close with:

1. Re-affirming commitment.
2. Agreeing on the next steps, including how you will complete the paperwork.
3. Scheduling follow-up meetings.

If completing paperwork is a mandatory part of the performance review process, aim to make it support the conversation. The conversation is where valuable information will emerge and the working relationship will continue to grow and prosper.

The paperwork cannot show you how truly engaged a person is but observing the person during a conversation can. Ask quality questions and pay attention to the person and what they say (and what they're not saying).

The paperwork cannot express or deal with the fears or concerns for the success or failure of a project. An open, honest conversation can.

The paperwork cannot explore alternatives and spark ideas for dealing with the more contentious work-related issues or short deadlines. An honest, two-way conversation can.

That said, the paperwork can capture the results of the conversation so support and follow-up can be given credibility and authority when seeking support or approvals at more senior levels or during negotiations across departments.

Paperwork detailing the results of the feedback conversation will also give you the specific examples you may need for the next feedback conversation.

◧ SALLY FOLEY-LEWIS

CHAPTER 9

PAY AND PERFORMANCE

Price is what you pay. Value is what you get.
– Warren Buffett

It's logical that your performance is linked to your remuneration. However, the conversations should not be linked. This is so the feedback conversation can focus on the person and their performance, not negotiations for pay rises.

When compensation and performance are handled in the same conversation, you risk the conversation merely becoming a tick-and-flick paperwork exercise. Such conversations typically only cover whether the person has met their goals and is eligible for a pay rise or bonus.

Yes, this means two separate conversations. The more you can talk about remuneration opportunities and performance separately yet regularly throughout the year, the easier the conversations will become and the more engaged employees will be. (*Harvard Business Review*, "Stop Basing Pay on Performance", 2014; "How To Discuss Pay with your Employees", 2014. These two articles include research and case studies that support this.)

If your organisation currently combines the performance review and compensation review in the one meeting, you need to separate it into two meetings. Ensure you support staff who facilitate these meetings. Inform them why you want to split the meetings and provide them with the necessary skills and guidance to roll out these conversations. Be prepared to communicate the change constantly until people have adjusted.

WHAT'S NEXT?

There are several points worth considering as you create better feedback conversations using the EECC feedback formula:

Quick Audit:

Take a moment to reflect on how effective your feedback conversations have been in the past. After using the EECC formula a few times, compare the quality of the conversations and ask others what they think about the quality.

Culture of Feedback:

Actively encourage feedback conversations. The more you ask for and give feedback using the EECC formula, the more embedded it will become in the organisation's culture.

Everyone Using the EECC:

Encourage all your colleagues, team members and employees to use the EECC formula. Share your copy of *Successful Feedback* with them – just be sure to get it back! Better still, buy them a copy each (shameless plug right there!).

But seriously …

When you're surrounded by other people who also use the EECC formula, you'll discover how smoothly and easily feedback conversations can and will flow. They become second nature. When the whole team understands the value of a thorough feedback conversation:

- Work becomes easier.
- Mistakes are fewer.
- Mistakes are quicker and cheaper to fix.
- Communication improves overall.
- Relationships are stronger.
- Staff are happier and healthier.
- Turnover reduces.
- Opportunities to improve work, value add, save money and even make money increase.

Training:

Everyone has their own preferred way to learn and develop. If you have a Human Resources or Learning and Development Department, it should be capable of helping you and your team develop the skills for successful feedback. If you want the whole team to learn how to use EECC, a workshop can be arrange, contact me at sally@sallyfoleylewis.com

A gem is not polished without rubbing, nor a man perfected without trials.
– Chinese Proverb

SALLY FOLEY-LEWIS

WANT MORE?

Sally Foley-Lewis is a productivity and leadership expert. She speaks, mentors and runs workshops to help leaders and dedicated professionals become exceptionally productive and confident leaders.

Sally writes a blog, produces the People and Management podcast, is the creator of self-coaching resource Management Success Cards®, and is the author of *The Productive Leader*.

Remember to also download your extra *Successful Feedback* resources: http://www.sallyfoleylewis.com/successful-feedback-extras/

To find out about Sally's resources, programs and workshops, go to www.sallyfoleylewis.com or connect with Sally on the following social media platforms:

LINKEDIN
www.linkedin.com/in/sallyfoleylewis/

TWITTER
twitter.com/SallyFoleyLewis

FACEBOOK
www.facebook.com/PeopleAndProductivity/

YOUTUBE
www.youtube.com/user/SallyFoleyLewis

Workshop – Flipped Feedback™

Flipped Feedback™ provides your leaders with the skills, knowledge and confidence to give and receive feedback to increase performance, motivate and engage their team.

1-day workshop

Learn more: http://www.sallyfoleylewis.com/flipped-feedback/

Ask Sally about the 360 Feedback 45-day blended program.

OTHER RESOURCES

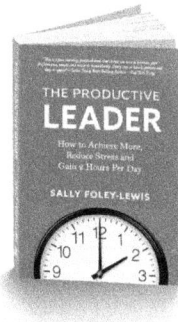

THE PRODUCTIVE LEADER
http://www.sallyfoleylewis.com/
book-the-productive-leader/

MANAGEMENT SUCCESS
CARDS®
http://bit.ly/MangtSuccessCards

PEOPLE AND
MANAGEMENT PODCAST

iTunes:
http://bit.ly/PeopleMantiTunes

Website:
http://bit.ly/PeopleMantWeb

Stitcher/Android:
http://bit.ly/PeopleMantStitcher

www.ingramcontent.com/pod-product-compliance
Lightning Source LLC
Chambersburg PA
CBHW072149020426

42334CB00018B/1927